P9-DFN-319

# JEFF GORDON

## Frank Moriarty

# MetroBooks

An Imprint of Friedman/Fairfax Publishers

©1999 by Michael Friedman Publishing Group, Inc.

All rights reserved. No part of this publication may be reproduced, stored in a retrieval system, or transmitted, in any form or by any means, electronic, mechanical, photocopying, recording, or otherwise, without prior written permission from the publisher.

Library of Congress Cataloging-in-Publication Data available upon request

ISBN 1-56799-851-8

Editor: Nathaniel Marunas
Art Director: Kevin Ullrich
Designer: Jonathan Gaines
Photography Editor: Sarah Storey
Production Director: Karen Matsu Greenberg

Printed in England by Butler & Tanner Ltd.

10 9 8 7 6 5 4 3 2

For bulk purchases and special sales,
  please contact:
Friedman/Fairfax Publishers
Attention: Sales Department
15 West 26th Street
New York, NY 10010
212/685-6610 FAX 212/685-1307

Visit our website:
http://www.metrobooks.com

# Contents

In the professional sports world, it's common to see stars. It seems like every team has one, the go-to guy fans count on to bring home victories. But superstars? That's another matter.

Superstardom is a level of achievement possibly awarded a bit too easily in these times when thousands of sporting events are broadcast every year. But a genuine superstar is someone who performs at a level that everyone can appreciate, whether you are a fan of that person's sport or not. These superstars become the names that define the sports they participate in. Think of names like Walter Payton and Joe Montana in football; Wilt Chamberlain and Michael Jordan in basketball; Arnold Palmer and Jack Nicklaus in golf; Mickey Mantle and Hank Aaron in baseball; Muhammed Ali and George Foreman in boxing; Gordie Howe and Wayne Gretzky in hockey—all of these athletes have become legends of their sports.

Motorsports has seen its share of superstars, drivers who bully or finesse their race cars, drivers who make the moves others fear to make, drivers who welcome the speed and danger that define their sport. The names of these legends of racing include the likes of Richard Petty, A.J. Foyt, Mario Andretti, Fireball Roberts, Al Unser, Johnny Rutherford, Bobby Allison, Dale Earnhardt, Bobby Isaac, and many more who have helped make motorsports incredibly popular.

In NASCAR, though, the 1990s are an especially exciting time. Stock car racing fans are getting that most special of opportunities—the chance to watch a legend being written before their very eyes. The man writing this legend is named Jeff Gordon. Though he has less than a decade of competition in NASCAR's elite Winston Cup Series, it's clear that Gordon is someone very special, someone with the talent and courage to earn the title that many observers have already bestowed upon him—superstar.

**Opposite page:** Intensity and focus are key elements of the package that has made Gordon a success in NASCAR's elite stock car racing series.

**Below:** Jeff Gordon has shown mastery of the unique skills required for superstardom in auto racing both in the close quarters of short track racing (seen here) and on the massive superspeedways.

# INTRODUCTION

**Pages 8-9:** The nimble handling of the light open wheel cars helped develop Jeff Gordon's lightning-fast reactions to racing situations. Here Gordon races in 1990 in Indiana with a USAC legend, the late Rich Vogler.

**Right:** At Ohio's famed Eldora Speedway in 1988, Gordon wrestles through a dirt turn. As Gordon demonstrates here, one of the unique cornering techniques of dirt track racing is to turn the wheels in the direction opposite to the one the driver wants the car to go in.

**Opposite page:** Gordon smiles for the camera in the Hoosier Dome, December 20, 1990. When it's too cold for midget racing in the Midwest, the competition moves indoors. Jeff seems pleased at the thought of challenging the small track on the stadium floor.

It was a day that everyone expected to be important, momentous even, and true to those expectations, November 15, 1992, was a milestone for NASCAR. It will be remembered as one of the most remarkable days in the history of stock car racing.

That Sunday offered a bounty of topics for motorsports journalists to write about and for race fans to ponder. Of course, on everyone's mind was the thrilling battle for the Winston Cup championship, which had come down to this very last race of the 1992 season. Davey Allison was the favorite, but Bill Elliott wasn't far behind in the points standings, and a studious young driver named Alan Kulwicki was also in the mix.

But this event at Atlanta Motor Speedway would also mark the final run for the King, Richard Petty. After a remarkable career that had seen Petty claim two hundred wins and seven championships, Richard was wrapping up his Fan Appreciation Tour and was poised to hang up his helmet.

The race itself was thrilling, one of NASCAR's greatest and most exciting. Davey Allison was caught up in a crash with Ernie Irvan and saw his championship hopes fade away. Bill Elliott chased Alan Kulwicki and finally took the lead, eventually winning the race. But Kulwicki had led the most laps, and—by carefully studying points mathematics—he knew that a second-place finish, coupled with a points bonus for leading the most laps, was good enough to win the 1992 championship.

Meanwhile, Petty's competitive laps ended with his car in flames, the result of an early race crash. The King came back for a ceremonial appearance at the end of the race, the final chapter of his legend having been written.

Despite all that was going on at Atlanta that day, before the green flag waved, those in the know cast

▪▪▪▪▪▪▪▪▪▪▪▪▪▪▪▪▪▪▪▪▪▪▪▪▪▪▪▪▪▪▪▪▪▪▪▪▪▪▪▪▪▪▪▪▪▪▪▪▪▪▪

**Opposite page:** At Winchester, Indiana's treacherous racetrack, Jeff prepares to compete in 1990. ESPN's short track Thunder broadcasts of midget and sprint car racing helped pave the way for Gordon's entry to stock car racing by making him a household name in racing.

**Below:** Jeff Gordon rockets around the Illinois State Fairgrounds in August 1989. Here he throws the car into a turn, letting the back end swing to set up a charge down the straightaway.

an eye to the twenty-first starting position. For there, in a Chevrolet Lumina bearing a rainbow of bright colors, was a young kid making his very first Winston Cup start. He had shaken up the Busch Grand National Series with blistering qualifying runs and strong race charges, and now here he was with the big boys. It didn't take long for all of the big boys of NASCAR racing to learn the kid's name—Jeff Gordon. Taking the green flag with stock car racing's biggest stars that day in 1992 was a young man whose dreams of racing had begun in California nearly two decades earlier.

Born in Vallejo, California, on August 4, 1971, Jeff Gordon was surrounded by the West Coast car

culture as a child. So it seems almost natural that, even as a young boy, Gordon set his mind on going fast. Aiding young Jeff's interest in speed was his stepfather, John Bickford. Bickford had married Jeff's mother, Carol, and introduced the family to racing by taking them to a local speedway when Jeff was less than a year old.

It wasn't long before Jeff expressed an interest in not just watching racing but trying his hand at it. After racing a bicycle that Bickford built for him to match his small stature, at just five years of age Jeff Gordon began to develop the talent that has led him to the Winston Cup Series. Bickford brought home quarter-midget cars—bought for $400—for Jeff and his sister, Kim. The young boy never looked back.

Quarter-midgets are the ideal introduction to race car driving for kids. Jeff's and Kim's quarter-midgets looked like the open-wheel race cars that roared around the dirt tracks of California, but they were scaled down in size and had single-digit-horse-power motors.

But even though the quarter-midgets were smaller and slower than the cars that older racers competed in, Jeff learned what competition was all about. He did crash from time to time, but he adapted to the sport at a pace that belied his age, zooming around a primitive track at fairgrounds in Vallejo. Soon it was time to race for real.

This photograph offers dramatic proof of Jeff Gordon's skills in open wheel competition. Here, at Salem Speedway in Indiana on June 17, 1990, Gordon has just won features in both the midget and sprint car divisions. Jeff and his stepfather, John Bickford, are flanked by car owner Rollie Helmling (left) and Bob East (right).

By the age of six, Jeff could boast thirty-five wins in main-event competition. He was a terror at qualifying, too, and it seemed as if no track records in his class were safe from his speedy assaults. His astonishing record in 1977 led to Gordon claiming the Western States championship and setting his sights on more competition.

Racing against competitors both his age and older in the years that followed, Gordon charged ahead at a scathing pace in quarter-midget racing. He began to compete outside of his native California and the results were the same. In 1978, he won forty-six quarter-midget races, then fifty-two the next year. By the time he was twelve years old, Jeff had racked up hundreds of victories and numerous championships. He'd even dabbled in go-kart racing, winning twenty-five kart races in 1981 alone.

It was clear to Bickford and to Jeff himself that it was time for a new challenge. So, at thirteen years of age, Jeff Gordon began sprint car racing.

Sprint car racing is the grassroots foundation of American oval-track competition. The cars are snarling, open-wheeled beasts with short wheelbases and lots of horsepower. They have always been considered the traditional stepping stone to Indy racing, so the idea of young hardchargers wanting to drive sprint cars was not new. But when the young hardcharger is just thirteen years old...well, that really was something new.

Jeff Gordon's attempt to enter the world of sprint car racing met with resistance, and he and Bickford spent considerable time arguing with worried track officials about Jeff's qualifications. But when he was given the chance, Gordon proved that he was the real thing. Of course, the wins didn't come as easily as they had in the quarter-midget days, but Gordon adapted quickly to the new level of competition.

Soon after Jeff's first win in sprint car racing at the KC Speedway in Ohio, his parents made a difficult decision. It was obvious racing could be more than just a hobby for their son. Jeff's potential seemed unlimited, and a successful career in motorsports seemed a realistic goal. But California is a long way from the dirt and paved tracks scattered throughout the Midwest, which is the heart of sprint

car racing. So John and Carol decided to gamble on the talents of their son.

In 1985, the Gordons moved to ground zero of United States Automobile Club racing—Indiana.

**Opposite page:** Open wheel racing has many traditions, and racing at Eldora Speedway is one of them. Gordon's performances at the Ohio track have added to the speedway's legend.

**Below:** One of open wheel racing's most prestigious events is the annual "Night Before the 500" race at Indianapolis Raceway Park, held on the eve of the Indianapolis 500. Here, in 1989, Gordon has just added his name to the elite list of winners of this race. The victory was also Gordon's first pavement-track USAC win.

# CHAPTER ONE

**I**n U.S. auto racing, the path had always seemed clear. Learn your driving skills and earn a reputation at your local track, then move up to USAC racing. Learn more, build a bigger reputation, and then—if you were lucky—it was on to glory, racing in the Indianapolis 500.

When Jeff Gordon's family moved to Indiana in 1986, it seemed that Jeff was following the same path so many USAC drivers had followed for decades to find fame and fortune in IndyCar racing. The assumption was natural because Gordon had an uncanny ability to get an open-wheel race car around an oval. Driving on a dirt track requires a racing approach unlike any other in motorsports—sometimes turning right when you want to go left, sliding the

**Pages 18-19:** Cutting his teeth in NASCAR racing, Jeff Gordon races alongside another future Winston Cup star, Bobby Labonte, as the two compete in a Busch Grand National race in 1992 at Charlotte Motor Speedway.

**Above:** This rare Tri-West High School (Lizton, Indiana) photo shows the young Jeff Gordon wearing a tie instead of a driver's suit.

**Right:** Gordon seems more at ease here in the pits in 1990, pondering tie rods rather than neckties. At the end of the season Jeff would claim the USAC Midget championship.

car's back end loose around the turn—and Jeff had that style down to a T.

But Jeff was also learning other important lessons in racing. Building relationships with other drivers helped shorten the learning curve, and seeing firsthand how important is the chemistry among members of a racing team was a crucial lesson.

One thing that Gordon did not need to learn was how to win. Despite the tougher level of competition in sprint car racing, Jeff still managed three wins in sixty feature races in 1986, and he also made an appearance racing sprint cars in Australia during the winter.

In part because of Jeff's globe-hopping racing schedule, his family faced tough times, barely eking out a living after their move from California. As John Bickford told *Newsweek*, the family "slept in pickup trucks and made our own parts. That's why I think Jeff is misunderstood by people who think he was born to rich parents and had a silver spoon in his mouth."

But when Jeff was granted a USAC license in 1987 at age sixteen—making him the youngest driver ever to obtain such a license—he was beginning to build up a reputation in the Midwest. In 1987, he enjoyed sixteen sprint car wins. More important, Jeff made his first starts with the World of Outlaws Series.

World of Outlaws cars are high-powered sprint cars with massive wings perched atop the roll cages, providing downforce as the cars blast through dirt track corners. More important, some of America's greatest race cars drivers were members of the WOO Series, and Jeff gained invaluable experience racing with the likes of Steve Kinser and Sammy Swindell.

By the time he graduated from high school in Pittsboro in 1989, Jeff Gordon had won track championships throughout the Midwest and notched wins in several USAC classes.

**Page 21:** In May 1991, Gordon celebrates a win at the Indiana State Fairgrounds track in the prestigious Hulman Hundred race for USAC Silver Crown cars. The Silver Crown cars are direct descendants of the legendary front-motor Indianapolis 500 race cars, and Gordon quickly took to the high-powered speedsters.

**Opposite page:** Pictured here is yet another type of open wheel car Jeff Gordon learned to master, the winged sprint car. The huge wing provides downforce in cornering, and seventeen-year-old Jeff Gordon has just used that stabilizing force to win his first USAC race, on May 20, 1989.

**Below:** Gordon sits at the wheel of the midget race car owned by Rollie Helmling, a car Jeff drove to his first USAC win on a pavement track.

That Gordon found time to pursue educational opportunities was important because drivers in modern professional racing need to present themselves well to a huge TV audience. And Jeff was already attracting national attention, as the growth of auto racing interest had drawn the cable television sports network ESPN to the Midwest to cover USAC and sprint car racing. Television loves a good story, and there wasn't a better one to be found than the tale of a friendly, intelligent, impossibly young driver who just loved to race.

In 1990, Jeff added another important credential to his growing racing résumé: he became the youngest Midget Series champion in USAC history.

"Driving at Indy or anywhere else is one thing, but racing is something else," three-time Indianapolis 500 winner Johnny Rutherford has said. "A good racer is always a good racer. If you want to make sure you're hiring a good racer, find someone who has won some midget and sprint car races." Jeff Gordon certainly met those qualifications, and as more and more race fans saw Jeff on TV, his name gained racing household status.

In years past, at this point in a racing career, a young driver would often make his first attempt at qualifying for the legendary Indianapolis 500, as Johnny Rutherford had once done. But times had changed. The Indianapolis 500 was now a stop on the CART (Championship Auto Racing Tour) Series, and IndyCars had become hideously expensive. A driver often had to supply his own big-dollar sponsorship in order to get a ride in CART, and foreign drivers competing in the Indianapolis 500 far outnumbered Americans.

In 1990, Jeff Gordon was at a motorsports career crossroads. He set his sights on stock car racing and NASCAR.

For years, NASCAR had been rapidly increasing in popularity. With the growth of cable television, NASCAR too had grown, and its fan base was increasing exponentially. The stock

**Opposite Page:** By 1990 Jeff Gordon had become well known through his performances in numerous races televised on ESPN, and the young driver was already attracting the attention of major sponsors.

**Left:** Even the most talented of budding superstars needs to make time for other activities…. Here, prom king Jeff Gordon stands proudly next to his queen, Deena Waters, in April 1989.

cars were safer than the fragile IndyCars, the money was good, and the television exposure was unbeatable. Going with NASCAR just made good sense.

"Right now, the way things have been going, if you're a young man and you're going to get into any form of racing to make a good living, and to make good money, then Winston Cup is the way you've got to go," Richard Petty said of NASCAR's attraction. "Used to be when you talked to these boys on Saturday night they wanted to go to Indy. But Winston Cup is the premier circuit in the world, where everybody talks about it and everybody points to it."

But before a young driver can reach the elite Winston Cup Series, an apprenticeship in the Busch

Grand National Series helps him learn the tracks and methodology of NASCAR racing. After Jeff attended the Buck Baker Driving School at North Carolina Motor Speedway in Rockingham, he felt it was time to test the NASCAR waters.

"The first time I got into a stock car, which was at a driving school, I loved it to death," Gordon recalled of his exposure to full-bodied race cars. "It felt right. I was just attracted to it right off the bat. And the opportunity came to me when I went to the driving school to drive a Busch car. I'd been to several other driving schools and no opportunity had ever come to me. It wasn't something that was planned, but it was something that I definitely wanted to do, and things came together and here we are

today. I wouldn't want to be in any other sport or any other type of division than Busch Grand National or NASCAR or Winston Cup."

Gordon's lessons at NASCAR legend Baker's school paid off. He tried to qualify for his first BGN race in 1990 at the same race track he had learned on, driving for car owner Hugh Connerty. When the field took the green flag, Jeff Gordon—in his first NASCAR start—was the second-fastest qualifier.

In 1991, Jeff added to his USAC record book, becoming the youngest-ever USAC Silver Crown Division champ, but he split his time with races on the Busch Grand National Series schedule, claiming Rookie of the Year honors in the latter.

"I think that the biggest difference is taking the step from open-wheel cars to the Busch cars," Jeff said of his transformation. Looking to the future he added, "I know it's going to be a big step to go from Busch cars to Winston Cup, but I don't think it's going to be as drastic as it was moving from open-wheel to Busch.

"Look at the difference of the cars—they're not even remotely close. You go from a 1,400-pound car with 700 horsepower and a whole lot of tire, and it handles completely different from these kind of cars that are 3,200-, 3,500-pound cars with about 500 horsepower. And Winston Cup cars are around 700 horsepower. It's been a big change."

But Jeff seemed to thrive on change. In 1992, he set his sights squarely on the Busch Grand National

Jeff Gordon poses with his wickedly powerful USAC Silver Crown car in August 1990 at Indiana State Fairgrounds. The huge rear tires help transfer the motor's tremendous power to the notoriously treacherous dirt surface of the speedway.

Series, driving a Ford Thunderbird for car owner Bill Davis. At just twenty-one years old, he scorched the series by winning the pole position as fastest qualifier eleven times, claiming three wins and finishing the season fourth in the championship points tally. Already Gordon could reflect on what he'd learned in the Busch Series and what he'd need to know in Winston Cup racing.

"I think learning the tracks, learning what the cars want and how to adjust them, and basically just how to drive the cars—I learned all last year, I took a full season just trying to figure that out," Jeff said during the 1992 Busch Grand National season. "Now this year we've really gotten to be pretty good at it on the Busch circuit. But I'm sure it's going to take a whole other year or two on the Winston Cup circuit to learn those cars."

**Opposite page:** A different series, but the same result—victory. Moving south from the USAC series to NASCAR racing, Jeff Gordon was quickly able to apply his racing skills to the bigger, heavier stock cars.

**Below:** Jeff Gordon drives to victory in a 1992 Busch Grand National race at Charlotte Motor Speedway, a pivotal moment in his career. A win at Charlotte alerts the Winston Cup community to a star on the horizon, and Gordon's star was definitely on the rise.

Pages 30-31: Jeff Gordon's first full season of Winston Cup racing found him switching from the Fords he drove in 1992 Grand National competition to the 1993 Chevrolet Lumina model.

Left: The birth of a legend: Jeff Gordon starts his first race in the NASCAR Winston Cup Series, at Atlanta Motor Speedway, November 1992.

Below: An unforgettable moment for any NASCAR driver is his first start in the Daytona 500. Jeff's first try at "The Great American Race" came in 1993, and he took home an impressive fifth place finish.

In 1992, Jeff Gordon was the twenty-one-year-old star of the Busch Grand National Series. His wins and pole positions were attracting a lot of attention. And when a Busch Series driver begins to build up big numbers, some of the most interested observers are the race team owners of the elite Winston Cup Series. After all, what team owner wouldn't want to be able to boast of recognizing the potential of the next racing superstar? With Busch Series races often running on the same tracks on the day before the Winston Cup races, team owners in NASCAR's top series are quick to hear about new Busch talent.

Gordon's aggressive Busch runs in Bill Davis' Thunderbirds were being observed and noted by a contingent of Winston Cup team owners. Among them was Rick Hendrick, a North Carolina businessman who had built a racing operation that fielded Winston Cup cars driven by Ken Schrader and Ricky Rudd.

Hendrick believed in the power of a multicar racing operation, but even more he believed in the talent of Jeff Gordon—especially after witnessing him

in action one Saturday at Atlanta Motor Speedway. Gordon seemed to be driving that day on the verge of losing control, pushing the car so aggressively that Hendrick was sure the young driver was about to crash. He never did, and Rick Hendrick decided almost on the spot to expand his Hendrick Motorsports operation to a three-car team for 1993 with a Chevrolet Lumina for Gordon.

When the news broke later in the season that Hendrick had signed Gordon, the stock car racing community was shocked. How had Ford Motor Company allowed a brilliant young driver like Jeff Gordon to slip through its fingers? The news was equally disturbing to Bill Davis, who had assumed that he, Gordon, and Ford were all going to make the leap to Winston Cup together. The bad feelings from the breakup lasted for years.

"Bill Davis and I don't have the relationship that we used to have," Jeff said late in 1995. "We got along real well, liked working together, but that

**Page 33 :** It can be a sobering experience for a young driver to suddenly find himself in the midst of Winston Cup's biggest stars, but Jeff Gordon quickly grew comfortable with the pressure-packed environment of NASCAR's top series.

**Opposite page:** Having won his very first Winston Cup pole position, Jeff Gordon has the honor of leading the field to the green flag at the October 1993 Winston Cup race at Charlotte Motor Speedway.

**Below:** Making friends with fellow drivers and getting advice on how to compete in the Winston Cup Series is an important part of every driver's entry to this level of competition. In the garage area at Talladega, Gordon relaxes with superspeedway master Ernie Irvan.

whole situation happened because I was forced to make a decision. I wanted to go Winston Cup racing the next year; I felt like that was the year for me to move on. I was needing to make a decision right then because I had some offers coming in to me. But I wanted to stick with Bill Davis. He had helped me

▪▪▪▪▪▪▪▪▪▪▪▪▪▪▪▪▪▪▪▪▪▪▪▪▪▪▪▪▪▪▪▪▪▪▪▪▪▪▪▪

**Opposite page:** The numbers 28 and 7 on the panel behind the window of Gordon's car memorialize Davey Allison and Alan Kulwicki, respectively, after their deaths in separate aircraft accidents in 1993. The loss of these two popular and talented young drivers made 1993, Gordon's rookie season, a somber year for everyone in the Winston Cup Series.

**Below:** Jeff Gordon celebrates winning a pole position (an impressive feat for a rookie competitor) with his mother (right) at Charlotte Motor Speedway, the heart of NASCAR racing.

get a good start in Busch Grand National, and Ford Motor Company had helped me out. I had Ford Motor Company telling me, 'Hey, we'll put you in a Ford whether it's Bill Davis or somebody else.' And I said, 'Well, who are you going to put me with?' They mentioned some teams, and they weren't teams that I felt were winning and they weren't teams that I felt were going to really improve and be something that was a good move for Jeff Gordon.

"Then, with the Bill Davis situation, we were just waiting to get a sponsorship. It's tough when you're somebody that has no experience as a driver, who's only twenty or twenty-one years old, and you have no experience as a car owner. We weren't really get-

ting any leads, we weren't getting any positive things to talk about. It just didn't seem like the sponsors were coming. I'd already been talked to by a couple of other Winston Cup owners. One of them was real positive, but when Rick Hendrick came along it just happened to be the right time. We were running out of time with Bill Davis, and it was a great opportunity that would have been difficult for me to turn down. Now I can say that I made the right decision and nobody can argue with me. But back then, it was the hardest thing I've ever had to do."

🏁🏁🏁🏁🏁🏁🏁🏁🏁🏁🏁🏁🏁🏁🏁🏁🏁🏁🏁🏁🏁

**Above:** Jeff brakes hard as he enters a turn at Martinsville Speedway in 1993, his first visit to that track as a Winston Cup driver. Jimmy Hensley follows in the number 7 Thunderbird he drove after Alan Kulwicki, the 1992 champion and owner of that Ford team, was killed just days before this race. The late Davey Allison, in one of his last races, closes in on Hensley.

**Opposite page:** Peer into the eyes of a champion-to-be. This 1993 photograph shows the rookie looking to the future and the glories to come.

Although Gordon finished out the 1992 Busch season driving for Davis, he made his first Winston Cup start for Hendrick Motorsports in the series' final event of the year. Gordon started the November 15 race at Atlanta Motor Speedway in the twenty-first position, but he fell from the race after his car was damaged. Gordon was credited with thirty-first in the final race results.

Was Gordon about to get the rude awakening to Winston Cup racing so many drivers have suffered through?

As Winston Cup driver Jimmy Spencer has noted, "I think anybody that's a champion and winning a lot of races in any division, whether it be in the Midwest or Southeast or the Northeast where I came from, then goes to a division that you are going to have a hard time qualifying for, running in the top twenty let alone the top ten.... It's a very traumatic experience in a way. A lot of people fail at it, a lot of people don't want to take the challenge."

Jeff Gordon was up to the challenge, and he proved it when his Du Pont–sponsored Lumina was unloaded beneath the bright Daytona, Florida, skies during Speedweeks of 1993. Not only did Gordon become the youngest driver to ever win a 125-mile (201km) Daytona 500 qualifying race, but in the 500 itself on February 14, Gordon raced to a fifth-place finish, beating out such drivers as Mark Martin, Sterling Marlin, Terry Labonte, and his Hendrick teammates Rudd and Schrader. Clearly, Jeff Gordon had arrived in the Winston Cup Series.

How did Gordon make such a fast start in his Winston Cup career?

"Probably because of Rick Hendrick's resources, and also because Ray Evernham went with me," Gordon reflected three years later. "I think that's been the key to a lot of the success, that if you look at when I was winning races in Busch Grand National, Ray was there, and since I've been in Winston Cup, Ray has been there. He and I just really work well together. And I think that not many rookies can come into Winston Cup and have the type of cars and the type of equipment and the resources and the people that I've been able to have at Hendrick's."

Gordon has always been quick to recognize the role Ray Evernham, his crew chief, has played in his advancements. Considered one of the best minds in

Jeff Gordon aims for his pit stall in 1993 at Atlanta Motor Speedway. In the years to come, the pits would be the place where Gordon won races, thanks to his exceptional pit crew, who came to be known as the Rainbow Warriors.

Winston Cup racing, Evernham was born in Red Bank, New Jersey, on August 26, 1957. He had grown up in the Northeast racing scene, and even tried his hand at driving the extremely fast Modifieds that are so popular in that part of the country.

But Evernham had decided that his skills were better suited to working behind the pit road wall rather than behind the wheel. From 1984 until 1989, he was crew chief and team manager for the International Race of Champions series, preparing cars for many of the world's greatest drivers. When he was first paired up professionally with Jeff Gordon on the Bill Davis Busch team, he found he was working with another great.

Evernham understood exactly what Jeff was going through in his race car and had a unique ability to communicate that helped Gordon mature quickly as a Winston Cup driver. Evernham's race preparation abilities were exceptional as well, and the entire crew of the number 24 car began to gel as a force to be reckoned with.

Adding to Jeff's Daytona success were second-place finishes in 1993 at the Coca-Cola 600 at Charlotte Motor Speedway and at the Miller 400 at Michigan International Speedway. There were seven top-five finishes and eleven top-tens. Gordon also drove to his first Winston Cup pole position in October at Charlotte. When the season came to a close, Jeff Gordon had handily beaten Bobby Labonte and Kenny Wallace for Winston Cup Rookie of the Year honors.

It had been a good year, one that created a foundation. But in 1994, Jeff was ready to build on that foundation.

"When we found out how good we were going to run in our first year, we thought, 'This is going to be great. We're going to get some experience, learn from these things, and hopefully great things are going to happen.'"

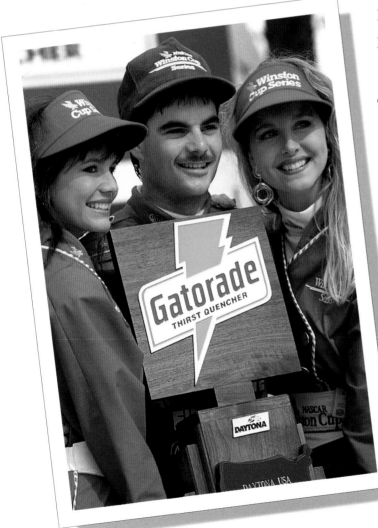

**Left:** Jeff Gordon celebrates at Daytona, having just won one of the 125-mile (200km) qualifying races for the 1993 Daytona 500. He may not have known it then, but he had also just met his future wife, Brooke Sealy (left), who served as Miss Winston in 1993.

**Opposite page:** A brilliant race-day strategist, crew chief Ray Evernham has become one of the most respected names in Winston Cup racing. Much of the credit for Jeff Gordon's success is due to Evernham's prerace preparation and his ability to react to situations that develop during competition.

# CHAPTER THREE

For some Winston Cup drivers, victory is an elusive goal. It may take years to capture a win in NASCAR's top division, and in some frustrating cases, the win may never come.

In the case of Jeff Gordon, though, the stock car world expected him to win not long after his 1993 rookie season. After all, the number 24 team seemed to have all the pieces put together—a daring and aggressive driver, a smart crew chief, the financial resources of a wealthy team owner, and a dedicated crew.

When the Winston Cup teams assembled in Daytona for the beginning of the 1994

**Pages 44-45:** After a solid rookie season, 1994 was a year for Jeff Gordon to run up front with the biggest names and brightest stars of Winston Cup racing.

**Above:** No longer Miss Winston, Brooke Sealy took her place at Jeff Gordon's side as his girlfriend (and later as his wife).

**Left:** The DuPont team rolls the number 24 Lumina through the garage area at Talladega Superspeedway.

**Opposite page:** His moustache gone in 1994, Jeff Gordon had proven to all that he could compete with the best drivers in NASCAR. He'd come close to winning in 1993; he was determined to reach victory lane in 1994.

season, Jeff Gordon quickly served notice that his team was ready to step up by finishing one position better in the Daytona 500 than he had the year before. Gordon swept home to a fourth-place finish, following winner Sterling Marlin, Ernie Irvan, and Jeff's new Hendrick teammate, Terry Labonte. The

**Opposite page:** Jeff Gordon follows Dale Earnhardt through a turn at Bristol Motor Speedway in 1994. Earnhardt won his seventh championship that season, but Gordon's time was coming.

**Below:** Jeff Gordon streaks across the start/finish line at Daytona International Speedway during the 1994 Daytona 500. Although Gordon leads his Hendrick Motorsports teammate Terry Labonte's number 5 at this point, Gordon finished the race in fourth, one position behind Labonte.

strong finish gave Gordon's team momentum moving into the long season schedule.

Jeff edged closer to victory lane at Richmond International Raceway in March, taking third on the heels of Rusty Wallace and winner Ernie Irvan.

In May, the Winston Cup Series arrived at Charlotte Motor Speedway for the all-star Winston Select race, followed a week later by NASCAR's longest race, the Coca-Cola 600.

Gordon quickly showed he was ready to make some noise at Charlotte, winning the qualifying race for the Winston Select and then taking the pole position as fastest qualifier for the 600. But nobody

expected young Gordon to win his first Winston Cup race in NASCAR's six-hundred-mile (965km) challenge. After all, that race was a grueling challenge that was traditionally won by a veteran with lots of endurance and experience.

On lap 375 of the four hundred laps around the 1.5-mile (2.41km) track, leader Rusty Wallace pitted for four tires. Those in close pursuit of Wallace did the same: Ernie Irvan, Dale Jarrett, and Geoff Bodine. And then, on lap 381, in came Gordon for his final pit stop. Ray Evernham had assessed the situation and made a brilliant call—make a two-tires-only pit stop. The time that Gordon saved in the pits made all the difference, as Jeff led Rusty Wallace to the finish line by almost four seconds. It was an emotional scene in victory lane as the 24 team celebrated a hard-earned victory in NASCAR's longest race.

The brilliant strategy invoked by Ray Evernham at Charlotte is just part of the reason Jeff relies so heavily on his crew chief.

"Ray is a lot like a coach; he's a great motivator and he's a good friend of mine," Gordon said, reflecting on their relationship. "I don't think our team could be as successful without him. He's been in a race car before and knows how to relate to what I'm saying. He's just the perfect kind of crew chief

**Left:** Where races are won and lost—the pits. Here, Gordon's speedy and efficient Rainbow Warriors return their driver to the track before the competing pit crews have completed their work, in what would become a common sight in pit row.

**Following pages:** Short track racing, as seen here at Martinsville Speedway in 1994, is the foundation of NASCAR racing. Jeff Gordon quickly became adept at manhandling the heavy Winston Cup cars through narrow turns in crowded conditions.

for me, and not every crew chief would be able to work with me. Because I'm the type of driver where I know what I feel and just relate back to the crew chief what I'm feeling and what I need in the car instead of knowing that if I'm feeling this, I need this, this and this in the car. Ray and I really just complement each other."

Gordon's team logged top-ten finishes in four of the next seven races. And then the Winston Cup Series traveled to Indianapolis for the highest-profile race of the year, the inaugural Brickyard 400.

The Indianapolis Motor Speedway had always symbolized racing in America, but the track had been the sole domain of the open-wheel IndyCars since the track's inception. In 1994, a new tradition was ready to be born when NASCAR's Winston Cup Series came to Indianapolis.

Every driver wanted to win the first Brickyard 400. An astonishing ninety cars tried to qualify for the forty-three starting positions. Jeff Gordon qualified very well and was poised to start the race from third position.

Under brilliantly sunny Indiana skies and comfortable temperatures, the Brickyard 400 field took the green flag on August 4, 1994. At first it appeared that Geoff Bodine might very well be the first Brickyard winner—until his brother Brett knocked him from competition in an accident.

As the race reached its closing stages, it became clear that there were two exceptionally strong cars:

The number 24 car runs at Darlington, adorned by a "doughnut," a mark created by another car's tire. Gordon quickly learned not to be intimidated by other drivers and isn't afraid to "trade paint" when necessary.

the Ford Thunderbird of Ernie Irvan and the Chevrolet Lumina of Jeff Gordon. The black Ford and the rainbow-colored Chevy swapped the lead back and forth as the crowd of 300,000 rose to their feet and cheered. And then, with five laps to go, Ernie Irvan suffered a flat tire. Jeff Gordon—in NASCAR's biggest race of the year, in front of the fans of his adopted home state—won the Brickyard 400.

*The Indianapolis Star*, in a special edition the next day, proclaimed Gordon's victory "a made-for-television script that would have left Walt Disney with a lump in his throat. Growing up a few minutes from the Indianapolis Motor Speedway, Gordon dreamed of racing there one day, and his debut was about as good as it gets."

"You can hit it right on one day, and we feel like that was our day at the Brickyard," Gordon said of the race. "It was like it was meant to be, like a fantasy that came true because we wanted it so bad."

**Above:** Wins like those in the 1994 Coca-Cola 600 in Charlotte and later at the Brickyard 400 made Gordon a natural for interviews, and his ability to handle those interviews with intelligence and ease was beneficial to NASCAR's move to prominence on the national sports stage.

**Opposite page:** Jeff Gordon pulls into victory lane at Indianapolis Motor Speedway for a storybook finish. He had just won the first Brickyard 400, in front of the fans of his adopted home state of Indiana.

Gordon had definitely established his credentials as a winner in the Winston Cup Series, and from the Brickyard the team went on to complete a season highlighted by twelve other top-ten finishes in addition to the two wins.

"We were trying to win a race that first year, and we came close and had a second a couple of times. The next step was to win a race," Gordon said of his sophomore season. "You make that your goal, and you think you can do it, but when it actually happens at this level it's amazing. That's why our emotions really showed when we won the Coca-Cola 600. And I don't think we could have gone and won the Brickyard if we hadn't first won the Coca-Cola 600. That was real exciting to win not just one race, but two of the biggest races on the circuit in our second year."

# CHAPTER FOUR

**Pages 58-59:** The precisely choreographed ballet of the pit stop, as performed by the Rainbow Warriors. Their countless hours of practice directly contributed to Jeff Gordon's first championship season.

**Left:** The 1995 Winston Cup campaign found the Chevrolet teams moving from the Lumina to the highly aerodynamic Monte Carlo.

**Below:** Now that he'd tasted victory in the Winston Cup Series, it was time for Jeff Gordon to build consistency and make a run at the series championship.

**Opposite page:** In a championship-caliber season, qualifying well is essential. Here, Jeff Gordon leads the field at the start of the second Brickyard 400 after capturing the pole in qualifying races.

fter Jeff Gordon and his Hendrick Motorsports team claimed wins in two of the biggest races of 1994, their fellow competitors were worried about just how strong the team would be in 1995. As it turned out, they had ample reason for concern.

At the season-opening Daytona 500, Gordon led sixty-one of the first ninety-one laps at the wheel of his new Monte Carlo. But a rare pit miscue—when Gordon's car slipped off the jack during a routine tire change—led to an uncharacteristically mediocre twenty-second-place finish.

A week later, Gordon and company made up for Daytona, qualifying on the pole at North Carolina Motor Speedway and then leading 329 of 492 laps on the way to Jeff's first win of 1995. He won again two weeks later at Atlanta Motor Speedway, then three weeks later at Bristol Motor Speedway. Gordon padded his championship quest with top-five finishes when he wasn't outright winning.

But winning was the focus of the season, and Jeff won his first major Daytona race on July 1 with a victory in the Pepsi 400. That was followed by wins in the season's second half at New Hampshire International Speedway, Darlington Raceway, and Dover Downs International Speedway. But most important, the number 24 team claimed an astound-

ing fourteen top-ten finishes in a row beginning at Michigan International Speedway on June 18. That is the kind of consistency that wins championships—and, when the checkered flag fell over the final race in November, Jeff Gordon was the 1995 NASCAR Winston Cup champion.

"Really, you want to go out there and win every race if it's possible—you want to try to at least do that," Gordon said of his championship season. "I

**Above:** The Hendrick Motorsports DuPont Monte Carlo tore through the 1995 season at such a torrid pace that even photographers had a hard time keeping up with the speedy Jeff Gordon.

**Opposite page:** Every driver in NASCAR racing longs to win the Southern 500, one of the most historic races on the schedule, at legendary Darlington Raceway. In 1995, it was Jeff Gordon's turn to win the Labor Day classic.

think that's what we did. We went out there and just tried to go to the front, tried to lead laps, and tried to win races. When we look back now, our bonus points from leading laps certainly paid off. I think that was a major contributor to the championship, and I think because we went out there trying to win and not just trying to finish bettered our finishes.

"But at the same time, when you do that you sometimes put yourself in a bad position, situations where you take extra chances that can cause you either problems or cause you to make mistakes on the race track. So it was one of those deals where we were aggressive, we were trying to win races, and when we realized that we had a shot at winning the championship, that's when we started to try to build the consistency a little more and had fourteen top-tens in a row."

**Pages 64-65:** *Brooke and Jeff Gordon chat before the start of one of the most grueling races of the Winston Cup Series schedule, at the high-banked, one-mile (1.6km) oval at Dover Downs International Speedway, in September 1995.*

**Above:** *At the 1996 Daytona 500, Dale Earnhardt jokes with Jeff Gordon. Things were more serious three months earlier, when Gordon had held off a determined charge from "The Intimidator" and claimed the 1995 Winston Cup Series championship.*

**Opposite page:** *By 1996, Jeff Gordon had already been proclaimed a superstar of stock car racing. But the young driver wasn't satisfied with just one championship—he was determined to do it again. He very nearly succeeded.*

What must have been especially satisfying to Gordon was that in order to win the championship, he held off a determined charge at the title made by the great Dale Earnhardt, who finished the season just thirty-four points behind Jeff.

"I thought it was a real privilege to be able to race with Dale and I respect him a whole lot," Gordon said. "He'd jab at me every once in a while trying to get me to loosen up and have fun, and I think he saw how focused I was and that I didn't really get into the fun. When he'd call me 'Wonder Boy' and things like that, I stuck to my own thing and didn't really mess around. But I had a great time this year. I didn't really see Dale being 'The Intimidator' off the race track, but he's always carrying that on the race track. Any time you're around him, if he's running good he's going to be tough to beat."

Dale tried his best to intimidate the youngster, but Gordon maintained his concentration and made his racing dream come true.

"To win a championship you've got to do it throughout the whole year," Gordon said of his achievement. "You can't just hit it every once in a while, you've got to hit it all the time and have the consistency—you can't fall out of races. After last year and the year before, I realized how difficult it is to win a championship. We're all the time trying to finish every race, finish as far forward as possible, knowing that the best we've done is eighth in the points in the past. To go out there and have a year like we did this year is amazing.

"I think other people look at it the same way. They think, 'OK, it's one thing for him to win races, but to be a champion, now that's something!' If you look back at how many people have won championships, you see it's pretty hard to come by. Only the guys that have been the best have gone on to win championships."

So outstanding was the performance of Gordon's crew that they were now known as the Rainbow Warriors, after the colors of Jeff's car and their fierce determination to make sure their driver had all the support he needed.

With championship in hand, the team set their sights on repeating the feat in 1996. But it was not to be. After winning the title in 1995, Gordon knew that consistency was the key element required to win

Preparation is the name of the game in Winston Cup racing. No one shows up at a race in ready-to-win condition. It takes hours of "dialing in" a race car to each track's unique characteristics. Jeff Gordon and his crew are among the best in the business at tailoring a car's setup to match conditions.

titles. But consistency in 1996 belonged to Terry Labonte, the quiet Texan who was Jeff Gordon's teammate at Hendrick Motorsports along with Ken Schrader. Labonte won the 1996 championship by thirty-seven points over teammate Gordon, supporting his two wins with nineteen additional top-five finishes. Labonte's season record in 1996 was racing consistency defined, and was good enough to win the title—even though Gordon won an amazing ten races in the season.

But those ten wins couldn't overcome two major breakdowns in the Du Pont team's seasonal assault. The first problem came right at the beginning of the season: back-to-back finishes at Daytona and Rockingham of forty-second and fortieth, respectively. Even that devastating start to the year couldn't stop Gordon, and after winning the final Winston

Cup race ever held at historic North Wilkesboro Speedway, he held a sizable 111-point lead over Terry Labonte with just four races left in the season.

Unfortunately, that's when the second troubling group of problems reared its head. At Charlotte, Jeff finished a dismal thirty-first. At Rockingham, the team had to settle for twelfth. Then came a fifth at Phoenix, and finally a third at Atlanta. In those same four races, Labonte came home in first, third, third, and fifth, respectively. That gave Labonte the points he needed to pass his Hendrick teammate and make off with the championship.

There were other factors at play, although admittedly they affected all of the competitors. Throughout the year, NASCAR had tinkered with the aerodynamic rules on the new Monte Carlos, trying to "balance the playing field" among the

Chevrolets, Pontiacs, and Fords. Gordon was proud of the work his team did to keep up with the changing rulebook.

"It's definitely a concern for Ray and the crew," Gordon noted. "They're the ones who, every time a rule change is made, they have to rethink the way they do things and try to get as much downforce out of the body that we're given by NASCAR as we can. That also relates to me because I'm the one who has to work around those changes. It's wild that you go from one race at one race track and the car is handling beautifully and feels great, and then you go back the next time and it's not the same because so many changes in the rules have been made."

Having fallen short of repeating as Winston Cup champions by the slimmest of margins, the Rainbow Warriors looked to 1997 with intensity. They had won ten races in 1996 and watched the championship slip away. It would not happen again. The crew was primed and their driver was hungry to conquer the series again.

"I know how special it is to be Winston Cup champion," Gordon said of his 1995 title. "It's something that I'll be able to remember and enjoy for the rest of my life, because every time they introduce me it's going to be as the 1995 Winston Cup champion. That's a great feeling. It's a great accomplishment and I'm very proud to be a part of it. I'm glad that my team could be a part of it.

"One thing about great champions in Winston Cup is that the truly great champions are the ones who have won more than one championship. That's something that is very, very hard to do. I'm very proud to be able to say that I've won one and it's quite an accomplishment, but to be able to say I've won more than one is something even greater."

🏁🏁🏁🏁🏁🏁🏁🏁🏁🏁🏁🏁🏁🏁🏁🏁🏁🏁🏁🏁🏁🏁🏁

**Above:** Winning one Southern 500 at Darlington can be the highlight of a driver's career; in 1996, Jeff Gordon made it two in a row, as wife Brooke and Ray Evernham attend to the victor after the long, hot race.

**Opposite page:** Seeking divine inspiration or just watching a passing aircraft? Both Ray Evernham and Jeff Gordon have credited their religious faith with helping them attain their goals in racing and in life.

 en wins in one season and no championship. It had happened to Rusty Wallace in 1993, and it happened to Jeff Gordon in 1996. Wallace had vowed to maintain that level of performance and win the championship the next year; instead, his win total went into a slow decline beginning in 1994. Would the same fate befall Gordon's Rainbow Warriors?

Ray Evernham took inspiration from a book by National Basketball Association coach Pat Riley. In the book, Riley outlined a plan for a five-step "Ladder of Evolution"

**Pages 72-73:** A dream comes true: the champagne flies as Jeff Gordon, winner of the 1997 Daytona 500, celebrates his victory in NASCAR's biggest race. It was to be the first win of a monumental season for the Rainbow Warriors.

**Above:** Although some say Jeff Gordon can do anything with a race car, the weather is out of his control. Here at the 1997 Winston 500, the old saying is proven true—"there's nothing sadder than a racetrack in the rain."

**Left:** In sunnier times, Gordon laughingly discusses the on-track handling characteristics of the DuPont Monte Carlo.

**Opposite page:** Gordon, seen here at the 1997 Brickyard 400, returned to Indianapolis Motor Speedway determined to become the first driver to win two Brickyard 400s. That distinction had to wait until 1998.

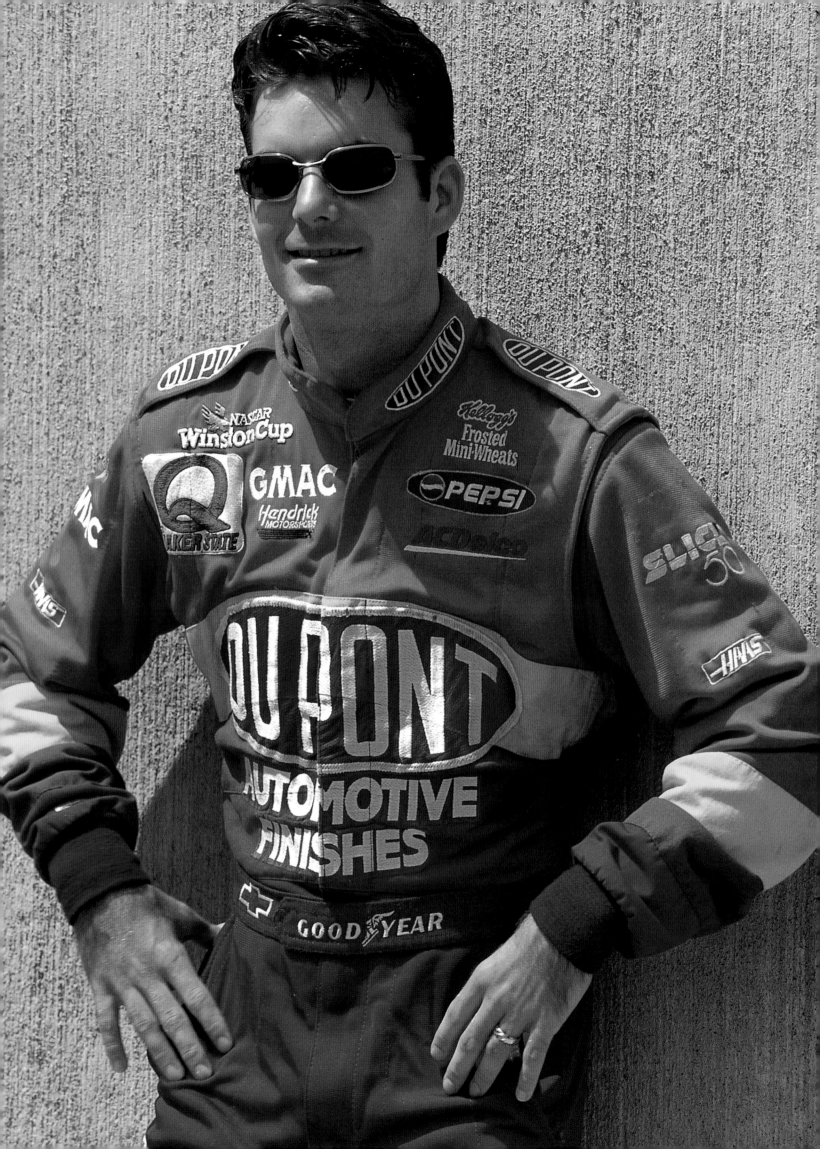

**Above:** *Jeff Gordon's success brought numerous endorsements his way as his fame grew, from a deal with Ray-Ban to backing from major cereal companies. Being associated with a winner is intelligent marketing.*

**Opposite page:** *The other pit crews are still servicing their race cars at Bristol Motor Speedway as Jeff Gordon heads back onto the track in 1997 action.*

that Evernham hoped to apply to Jeff Gordon and the Rainbow Warriors:

- From nobody to upstart
- From upstart to contender
- From contender to winner
- From winner to champion
- From champion to dynasty

An inspired 24 team showed they were still strong the week before the season-opening Daytona 500, winning the Busch Clash race for the fastest 1996 qualifiers. But that race was a non-points short event—nice to win but nothing that would help secure the 1997 championship. The Hendrick team was focused on the Daytona 500.

Late in the classic five-hundred-mile (804.5km) race, Bill Elliott was leading Gordon and both of Jeff's Hendrick Motorsports teammates, Terry Labonte and Ricky Craven. Elliott, the popular Georgia driver of Ford Thunderbirds, must have had a sense of foreboding when he looked in his rearview mirror and saw the fleet of Hendrick Chevrolets breathing down his back bumper. On lap 195 of two hundred, Elliott's fears came true as Gordon dipped low and Labonte and Craven rode high; all the Hendrick cars passed the lone Ford and took over the top positions.

On the last lap, the caution flag came out and the race ended under the yellow. It was an unprecedent-

ed sight to see three cars owned by the same owner take the top spots of the Daytona 500, and Jeff Gordon was ecstatic to have won NASCAR's most legendary race.

But the celebration had a poignant moment, as Gordon was forced to celebrate with his team owner

▪▪▪▪▪▪▪▪▪▪▪▪▪▪▪▪▪▪▪▪▪▪▪▪▪▪▪▪▪▪▪▪▪▪▪▪▪▪▪▪▪▪▪

**Pages 78-79:** The rainbow-colored Chevrolet has become one of the most popular cars in Winston Cup racing—as well as one of the most hated. The cheers of Jeff Gordon's fans frequently compete with the boos of his jealous detractors.

**Above:** Jeff Gordon and his Hendrick Motorsports teammates, Terry Labonte (left) and Ricky Craven (right), send a special "get well" wish to their colleague from Daytona's victory lane. The three Hendrick teams, led by Gordon, swept the top three positions in the 1997 Daytona 500.

**Opposite page:** In the high-pressure world of Winston Cup racing, a quiet consultation between Ray Evernham and Jeff Gordon is a precious commodity.

from victory lane using a cellular telephone. Rick Hendrick, the man who had provided Jeff Gordon with the tools he needed to ascend to the upper echelon of NASCAR, was at home in North Carolina, suffering from the effects of his treatment for the leukemia that had been diagnosed months before.

Not only did Jeff dedicate the win to Hendrick, but he and the race team dedicated their season to increasing awareness of the importance of bone marrow donations to battle the disease that had struck both Hendrick and crew chief Ray Evernham's young son.

Gordon's team moved on to the second race of the season, at North Carolina Motor Speedway, and powered past Dale Jarrett to win again. The team was on its way, combining the winning runs of 1996 with the championship-winning consistency of 1995. Victories came to Gordon at Bristol Motor Speedway, Martinsville Speedway, Charlotte Motor Speedway, Pocono International Raceway, the brand-new California Speedway, Watkins Glen International, Darlington Raceway, and New Hampshire International Speedway.

The 24 team won ten races in 1997—matching their total from 1996—and they accomplished their feat at ten radically different race tracks, a testament to preparation and skill. Jeff Gordon also became only the second driver to win the Winston Million $1,000,000 bonus for capturing three of the sport's most prestigious races in a single season. But most important, Jeff Gordon was crowned the 1997 Winston Cup champion, his second championship in three years.

Jeff Gordon is on top of the NASCAR world, and he knows he has been blessed by his success. That's why he works hard to increase awareness of organizations like those that battle leukemia.

"When things are going well for you and couldn't be going much better, then you realize that there are other people out there that aren't so fortunate," Gordon said of his work outside racing. "And children especially, they are the future, our future of America—maybe they aren't getting those opportu-

*Opposite page:* Jeff Gordon contemplates the handling of his Monte Carlo at Darlington in 1997. Despite his somber looks here in practice, Jeff went on to win his third straight Southern 500 that year (he won the historic event yet again in 1998). Darlington is known as the track that is "too tough to tame"–unless you are Jeff Gordon.

*Below:* A walk down pit road without at least one interview request is nearly unimaginable for a driver who has risen to the stature of Jeff Gordon.

nities that you're getting. If you can show other people out there that if you contribute you can save lives today, it means a lot to me and I hope I can help get the word out to others. Me, by myself, I can not contribute enough money—even as much money as I make, if I contributed everything it wouldn't be enough to make a difference. So that's why I like to try to do as much as I can, but also get the word out to many other people also."

Jeff's wife, Brooke, joins him in many of his activities. A former Miss Winston—one of the beau-tiful young women who present winning drivers with trophies in victory lane—Brooke first met Jeff in Daytona in 1993, after Gordon won one of the 125-mile (201.13km) qualifying races for the Daytona 500. A professional model who also worked as a licensed insurance agent, Brooke began her stint as Miss Winston late in 1992. Although drivers are not supposed to strike up relationships with any of the Miss Winstons, the beautiful representative of the Winston Cup sponsor and the dashing young driver made a storybook couple. After Brooke resigned from her Winston duties and the relationship became public knowledge, Brooke and Jeff were married and set up house near Lake Norman in North Carolina.

But all has not been perfect for the Gordons. In July 1998, it was announced that the Gordons were leaving their Lake Norman home to move to Florida.

Intrusive race fans had several times blocked access to the Gordon home, and Brooke even told *Sports Illustrated* that she had seen fans videotaping the family cat through a window of their home.

Gordon's relationship with the fans is complicated by his immense popularity. Although he tries hard to be accommodating when possible, and he has many thousands of loyal followers, there are many other race fans who inexplicably feel that what Jeff has earned came to him too easily. Signs bearing messages such as "Anybody but Gordon" are becoming as prominent in the speedway infields as similar signs referring to Dale Earnhardt once were. And, of course, when Jeff wins, that means all the fans of the other drivers are going home disappointed. The loud boos that greet Gordon's name during prerace driver introductions sometimes rival the enthusiastic cheers.

The jealousy of the anti-Gordon race fans and some fellow competitors who dislike Gordon probably stems more from jealousy over the success of his team rather than dislike for Jeff personally. After all, the Gordon team is one of the most dominant in recent years, but Gordon himself is honest, likable,

**Above:** Once he had mastered the ovals of Winston Cup racing, Gordon began to hone his skills on road courses. Here at the 1997 race at the course in Sonoma, California, Jeff placed second to Mark Martin. In 1998 he won the event.

**Opposite page:** By 1997, many people in the sport began to Gordon might be poised to break records that were once th Gordon's career got off to such a strong start so quickl almost no NASCAR record is safe.

and a wonderful representative of modern NASCAR racing.

As Gordon's popularity rises, though, the difficulty of staying focused grows.

"I think organizing my schedule is going to be the most important thing so that I'm not too strung out and doing too many things," Gordon admitted. "Really, I've never had a problem with that in the past. When you get in the race car, you shut off all of those outside things and all you think about and all you focus on is that race car."

The success that Gordon has had doing just that is inarguable, and his future in the sport seems unlimited. And, characteristically seeking to give something back to the sport, in July 1998, Jeff and Ray Evernham announced that they had formed Gordon-Evernham Motorsports, with the intention of running a full-time Busch Grand National car in the future to give another young driver the break he needs to make his mark on NASCAR racing.

**Opposite page:** Although Jeff didn't win the 1998 Daytona 500, the first race of the season, he made up for it by winning the season's second, the Goodwrench 400, at North Carolina Motor Speedway. Many more wins were to come that season.

**Below:** Jeff Gordon fell just short in the 1998 Daytona 500, but he was on the verge of another exceptional season that would leave the competition shaking their heads in frustration.

In 1998, Gordon and his team mounted a charge on a second consecutive championship, the third in four years.

At the Daytona 500 the 24 car was shuffled back in the hectic final laps in a race that ended under caution. The race also ended Dale Earnhardt's long years of frustration in attempts to win NASCAR's biggest race, as "The Intimidator" drove his black Monte Carlo to victory lane.

But the Rainbow Warriors would not have to wait long to taste victory. The very next week, at North Carolina Motor Speedway, Gordon and the Hendrick team made a statement about their championship hopes with a convincing win. The following week Mark Martin was the winner in Las Vegas,

the first NASCAR Winston Cup victory for the new Ford Taurus. At first it seemed that Gordon and Martin were just two of several top contenders for the title, but as the season unfolded names like Jeremy Mayfield, Jeff Burton, Rusty Wallace, and finally Dale Jarrett fell from title contention.

In the end, it came down to a battle between Martin and Gordon.

Mark Martin's midseason performance was an impressive one, as he drove his Roush Racing Taurus to wins at the California 500, the Miller Lite 400 in Michigan, the Goody's 500 in Bristol, Tennessee, and the MBNA 400 in Dover, Delaware. When he wasn't winning, he was scoring top five finishes. It must have been incredibly frustrating to see Jeff

**Above:** The consummate NASCAR team for the twenty-first century: Jeff and Brooke Gordon (seen here at Pocono International Raceway for the running of the 1998 Pocono 500).

**Opposite page:** The motto of stock car racing–"go fast, turn left"–has been taken to heart by Jeff Gordon, and with each season he threatens to rewrite the record books of NASCAR.

Gordon performing just slightly better week after week. No matter how well Martin's team did, Gordon's seemed to do better. During the period Martin won those four races, Gordon won eight.

The frustration boiled over late in the season when Martin's car owner, Jack Roush, demanded an inspection by NASCAR for illegal tire additives, an action interpreted by many as an outright accusation that Gordon's team was cheating. An investigation by the sanctioning body determined that there were no illegal activities—Gordon's success was solely due to outstanding performances.

The key to the championship were the back-to-back races in October at the fearsome superspeedways in Talladega, Alabama, and Daytona Beach, Florida. Martin traveled to Alabama with seven wins, but trailed Gordon by more than 100 points in the standings. Jeff already had another ten wins, but many in the media were quick to point out that if Gordon was caught up in one of the characteristic multicar crashes at either superspeedway race, then Martin would be right back in close title contention.

Instead, the superspeedway races became the final blow to Martin's hopes. It was Mark who was caught up in the big wreck at Talladega, while Jeff drove on to finish second. A week later Gordon captured the Daytona night race for his eleventh victory of the season. Gordon clinched the 1998 Winston Cup Series championship with yet another first-place finish, at the AC Delco 400.

But no matter how many championships Jeff Gordon eventually wins over the course of his career, they will only add to the amazing story of a born racer who blazed his own trail to NASCAR Winston Cup superstardom.

"I would never have dreamed it—I had no clue that racing would ever lead me to what it has and the opportunities and the things that I do now," Gordon has said of his career. "It's amazing. I never thought that people would stand in line to get an autograph from me. I never had any idea that racing would lead to this, that it would be my career, the thing that I do for the rest of my life."

**Opposite page:** Jeff Gordon goes through a last-minute, prerace check with the crew in 1998 before one of the biggest races of any NASCAR season, the Daytona 500.

**Above:** Jeff Gordon's future seems almost impossibly bright—who knows how many wins, how many championships, will grace his résumé once his career is over....